NORTH AMERICA

GREENLAND
(DENMARK)

NUNAVUT

Hudson
Bay

NEW FOUNDLAND

MANITOBA

QUEBEC

CANADA

ONTARIO

HEWAN

NORTH
DAKOTA

MINNESOTA

Great Lakes

P.E.I.

NEW
BRUNSWICK

NOVA
SCOTIA

MAINE

Ottawa

VERMONT

NEW HAMPSHIRE

WISCONSIN

MICHIGAN

NEW YORK

MASSACHUSETTS
RHODE ISLAND
CONNECTICUT

SOUTH
DAKOTA

REAT

NEBRASKA

IOWA

ILLINOIS

INDIANA

OHIO

PENNSYLVANIA

NEW JERSEY

DELAWARE

MARYLAND

Washington DC

ATLANTIC OCEAN

STATES

KANSAS

MISSOURI

WEST
VIRGINIA

VIRGINIA

ADO

LAINS

OKLAHOMA

KENTUCKY

NORTH CAROLINA

SOUTH CAROLINA

Bermuda
(UK)

CO

TEXAS

ARKANSAS

TENNESSEE

ALABAMA

GEORGIA

MISSISSIPPI

LOUISIANA

FLORIDA

Rio Grande

Mississippi River

Missouri River

Mississippi River

Gulf of Mexico

MEXICO

Mexico City

THE
BAHAMAS

Nassau

Havana

CUBA

Turks & Caicos
Islands
(UK)

Virgin Islands
(US & UK)

Anguilla
(UK)

ANTIGUA &
BARBUDA

DOMINICAN
REPUBLIC

ST KITTS
& NEVIS

Guadeloupe (FRANCE)

DOMINICA

HAITI

Port-au-
Prince

Santo
Domingo

Puerto
Rico
(US)

Roseau

ST LUCIA

Martinique (FRANCE)

Cayman
Islands (UK)

Kingston

JAMAICA

ST VINCENT &
THE GRENADINES

BARBADOS

Bridgetown

GRENADA

Port of Spain

TRINIDAD &
TOBAGO

Caribbean Sea

Netherland Antilles
(NETH)

Aruba (NETH)

BELIZE

Belmopan

GUATEMALA

HONDURAS

Tegucigalpa

Guatemala City

NICARAGUA

San Salvador

EL

Managua

SALVADOR

San José

COSTA RICA

Panama
Canal

Panama City

PANAMA

N

W E

S

3

Caribbean Sea

VENEZUELA

Caracas

Georgetown
Paramaribo
GUYANA
SURINAME
Angel
Falls
Caye
Fre
Gui
(FRA)

COLOMBIA

Bogotá

AMAZON

RAIN

FOREST

Amazon River

Quito

ECUADOR

Galapagos
Islands
(ECUADOR)

A
N
D
E
S

PERU

BRAZIL

Lima

PACIFIC

Lake
Titicaca
La Paz

BOLIVIA

Sucre

GO

OCEAN

PARAGUAY

Asunción

CHILE

Easter
Island
(CHILE)

Juan Fernández
Islands
(CHILE)

Santiago
+Mt Aconcagua

URUGUAY

A
N
D
E
S

M
T
N
S

Buenos Aires

Montevideo

ARGENTINA

STOP

Falkland
Islands
(UK)

SOUTH AMERICA

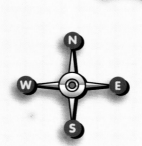

ATLANTIC OCEAN

Brasilia

South
Georgia
(UK)

5

Mediterranean Sea

Algiers
Tunis
TUNISIA
Tripoli
Rabat
MOROCCO
Madeira Islands (PORTUGAL)

Canary Islands (SPAIN)

ALGERIA
LIBYA

WESTERN SAHARA
(SOVEREIGNTY UNDETERMINED)
S A H A R A

MAURITANIA
Nouakchott
MALI
D E S E R

Dakar
SENEGAL
Banjul
THE GAMBIA
GUINEA-BISSAU
Bissau
GUINEA
NIGER
Niamey
CHAD
N'Djamena

Bamako
Ouagadougou
BURKINA FASO
BENIN
NIGERIA
Abuja

Conakry
SIERRA LEONE
Freetown
CÔTE D'IVOIRE
TOGO
GHANA
LIBERIA
Monrovia
Yamoussoukro
Accra
Porto Novo
Lomé
CENTRAL AFRIC REPUBLIC
Bangui

Gulf of Guinea
Malabo
CAMEROON
Yaoundé
EQUATORIAL GUINEA
SÃO TOMÉ & PRÍNCIPE
São Tomé
Libreville
CONGO
GABON

Ascension (UK)
DEMOCRA REPUBLI OF THE CONGC
Brazzaville
Kinshasa

Luanda

ATLANTIC

St Helena (UK)

ANGOLA

OCEAN

NAMIBIA
Windhoek

SOUT AFRIC

Cape Town

CAPE VERDE
Praia

GO

STOP

6

Cairo
Suez Canal
EGYPT

Red Sea

Nile River

Khartoum

ERITREA
Asmara

SUDAN

DJIBOUTI
Djibouti

Addis Ababa

ETHIOPIA

SOMALIA

Mogadishu

UGANDA
Kampala
Lake Victoria
KENYA
Kigali
RWANDA
Nairobi
Bujumbura
BURUNDI
Mt Kilimanjaro

TANZANIA

Dar es Salaam

N
W E
S

Victoria
SEYCHELLES

INDIAN OCEAN

MALAWI
Lilongwe

ZAMBIA

Lusaka

Harare

MOZAMBIQUE

Moroni
COMOROS

Mayotte
(FRANCE)

Mozambique Channel

MADAGASCAR
Antananarivo

ZIMBABWE
TSWANA

...borone

Maputo

...oria
Mbabane
SWAZILAND

...fontein
Maseru
LESOTHO

Réunion
(FRANCE)

Port Louis
MAURITIUS

ICELAND
Reykjavik

Norwegian Sea

Faroe Islands
(DENMARK)

Shetland Islands
(UK)

ATLANTIC OCEAN

SCOTLAND

NORTHERN
IRELAND

Dublin
IRELAND

UNITED
KINGDOM

WALES   ENGLAND

London

NETHERLANDS
Amsterdam
The Hague

Brussels
BELGIUM

Paris

LUXEMBOURG
Luxembourg

FRANCE

Bern
SWITZERLAND
Mont Blanc

LIECH.

A
L
P
S

MONACO

ANDORRA
PYRENEES

PORTUGAL   Madrid
Lisbon

SPAIN

Balearic Islands
(SPAIN)

North Sea

NORWAY
Oslo

Stockholm

SWEDEN

FINLAND

Helsinki

Baltic Sea

Tallinn
ESTONIA

Riga   LATVIA

LITHUANIA
Vilnius

RUSSIA   Minsk

BELARUS

DENMARK
Copenhagen

Berlin

GERMANY

Prague
CZECH
REPUBLIC

Vienna

POLAND   Warsaw

SLOVAKIA
Bratislava

Budapest

AUSTRIA   HUNGARY

SLOVENIA
Ljubljana   Zagreb
CROATIA

BOSNIA &
HERZEGOVINA
Sarajevo

SAN MARINO

ITALY

Corsica
(FRANCE)

VATICAN CITY   Rome

Sardinia
(ITALY)

UKRAINE

Kie

MOLDO
Chis

ROMANIA

Bucharest

Danube River

BELGRADE
SERBIA
AND
MONTENEGRO

BULGARIA
Sofia

Skopje
MACEDONIA

Tirane
ALBANIA

Danube River

Adriatic Sea

Tyrrhenian Sea

Mediterranean

Sicily
(ITALY)

Valetta
MALTA

GREECE

Aegean Sea

Athens

Crete
(GREECE)

Sea

GO

STOP

8

URAL MTNS

R U S S I A

Moscow

Volga River

lack Sea

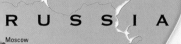

ARCTIC
OCEAN

ATLANTIC OCEAN

Lapt
Se

Barents
Sea

Kara Sea

U
R
A
L

M
T
N
S

RUSSIA

Black Sea

Ankara

TURKEY

GEORGIA
ARMENIA
Mt Ararat
AZERBAIJAN
Tbilisi
Yerevan
Baku

Caspian Sea

Astana

KAZAKHSTAN

Aral
Sea

UZBEKISTAN

Bishkek

Tashkent

KYRGYZSTAN

Nicosia

CYPRUS
LEBANON
Beirut
Damascus
Jerusalem
ISRAEL
Dead Sea
JORDAN

SYRIA

Amman

Baghdad

IRAQ

Tehran

TURKMENISTAN

Ashgabat

Dushanbe

TAJIKISTAN

Kabul

H
I
M
A
L
A
Y
A

KUWAIT

SAUDI
ARABIA

Kuwait City

IRAN

AFGHANISTAN

Islamabad

Manama
BAHRAIN
Doha
QATAR

Riyadh

Abu Dhabi

UNITED ARAB
EMIRATES

Muscat

PAKISTAN

New Delhi

NEPAL
Mt Everest
Kathmandu
BHUTAN
Th

Red Sea

BANGLADESH

Dhaka

OMAN

INDIA

Sanaa

YEMEN

Arabian
Sea

Bay o
Benga

Socotra
(YEMEN)

Lakshadweep
(INDIA)

Andaman Is
(INDIA)

Nicobar Is
(INDIA

SRI
LANKA

Colombo

Male

MALDIVES

INDIAN   OCEAN

Chagos
Archipelago
(UK)

GO

STOP

10

ASIA

East Siberian Sea

Sea of Okhotsk

MONGOLIA
aanbaatar

Sea of Japan

JAPAN
Tokyo

NORTH KOREA
Pyongyang
Seoul
SOUTH KOREA

GOBI DESERT
Beijing

CHINA
Yangtze River

East China Sea

PACIFIC OCEAN

Taiwan

YANMAR (BURMA)

LAOS
Hanoi
Hainan (CHINA)
gon oon)
Vientiane

PHILIPPINES
Manila

AILAND
Bangkok

VIETNAM
CAMBODIA
Phnom Penh

South China Sea

Celebes Sea

Bandar Seri Begawan
BRUNEI

Kuala Lumpur
MALAYSIA

SINGAPORE

INDONESIA

Banda Sea

Arafura Sea

Java Sea

Jakarta

Northern
Mariana
Islands
(US)

Guam
(US)

PALAU
• Koror

Palikir

FEDERATED STATES OF MICRONESI

PAPUA NEW GUINEA
+ Mt Wilhelm

SOLOMON
ISLAND

Port Moresby

Timor
Sea

Gulf
of
Carpentaria

Great Barrier Reef

Coral
Sea

NORTHERN
TERRITORY

QUEENSLAND

AUSTRALIA

+ Ayers Rock

WESTERN
AUSTRALIA

SOUTH
AUSTRALIA

Darling River

NEW
SOUTH
WALES

Canberra
CAPITAL
TERRITORY

Murray River

VICTORIA

Tasma

Tasman

TASMANIA

GO

STOP

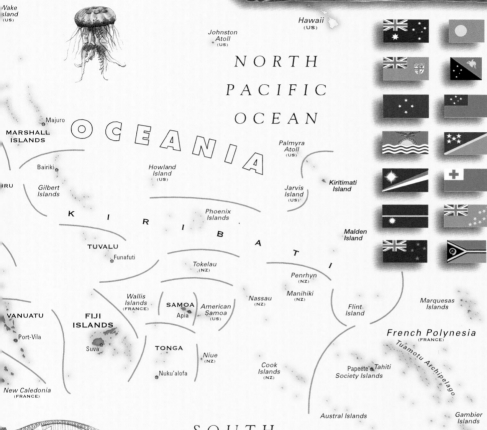

AUSTRALIA
AND THE REGION OF OCEANIA

Midway
Island
(US)

Wake
Island
(US)

Hawaii
(US)

Johnston
Atoll
(US)

NORTH

PACIFIC

OCEAN

OCEANIA

Majuro

MARSHALL
ISLANDS

Palmyra
Atoll
(US)

Bairiki

RU

Gilbert
Islands

Howland
Island
(US)

Jarvis
Island
(US)

Kiritimati
Island

K   I   R   I   B   A   T   I

Phoenix
Islands

TUVALU

Funafuti

Tokelau
(NZ)

Malden
Island

Penrhyn
(NZ)

Wallis
Islands
(FRANCE)

SAMOA

Nassau
(NZ)

Manihiki
(NZ)

VANUATU

FIJI
ISLANDS

American
Samoa
(US)

Flint
Island

Marquesas
Islands

Port-Vila

Suva

Apia

TONGA

Niue
(NZ)

Cook
Islands
(NZ)

French Polynesia
(FRANCE)

New Caledonia
(FRANCE)

Nuku'alofa

Papeete Tahiti
Society Islands
(NZ)

Tuamotu Archipelago

Austral Islands

Gambier
Islands

SOUTH

PACIFIC

OCEAN

ea

Kermadec
Islands
(NZ)

Pitcairn
Island
(UK)

NEW
ZEALAND

Wellington

Chatham
Islands
(NZ)

Auckland Islands
(NZ)

The Polar Regions

The North Pole

The map shows: UNITED KINGDOM, SWEDEN, NORWAY, FINLAND, ICELAND, Norwegian Sea, Jan Mayen (NORWAY), Greenland Sea, Labrador Sea, Barents Sea, Svalbard (NORWAY), GREENLAND (DENMARK), Baffin Island, Novaya Zemlya, Franz Josef Land, Baffin Bay, Kara Sea, Ellesmere Island, Hudson Bay, Severnaya Zemlya, North Pole, RUSSIA, ARCTIC OCEAN, CANADA, Laptev Sea, Victoria Island, New Siberian Islands, Banks Island, East Siberian Sea, Beaufort Sea, Wrangel Island, Chukchi Sea, UNITED STATES, Bering Strait, Bering Sea, ARCTIC CIRCLE

The South Pole

The map shows: ATLANTIC OCEAN, ANTARCTIC CIRCLE, South Orkney Islands, QUEEN MAUD LAND, ENDERBY LAND, INDIAN OCEAN, South Shetland Islands, Weddell Sea, Berkner Island, Amery Ice Shelf, ANTARCTIC PENINSULA, Ronne Ice Shelf, PENSACOLA MTNS, Alexander Island, TRANSANTARCTIC MOUNTAINS, Bellingshausen Sea, Vinson Massif, ELLSWORTH MTNS, South Pole, WILKES LAND, MARIE BYRD LAND, Ross Ice Shelf, Mt Erebus, PACIFIC OCEAN, Ross Sea, ANTARCTIC CIRCLE, Balleny Islands

14

ANTARCTICA
AND THE POLAR REGIONS

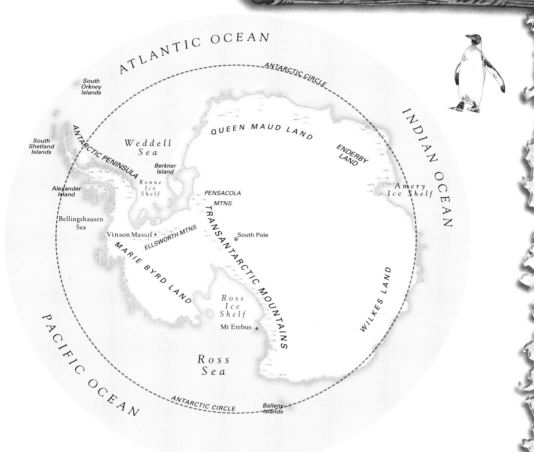

ATLANTIC OCEAN

ANTARCTIC CIRCLE

South Orkney Islands

South Shetland Islands

ANTARCTIC PENINSULA

Weddell Sea

QUEEN MAUD LAND

ENDERBY LAND

Berkner Island

Ronne Ice Shelf

Alexander Island

PENSACOLA MTNS

Amery Ice Shelf

Bellingshausen Sea

Vinson Massif +

ELLSWORTH MTNS

TRANSANTARCTIC MOUNTAINS

⊕ South Pole

INDIAN OCEAN

MARIE BYRD LAND

Ross Ice Shelf

Mt Erebus +

WILKES LAND

PACIFIC OCEAN

Ross Sea

ANTARCTIC CIRCLE

Balleny Islands

15

The Seven Continents

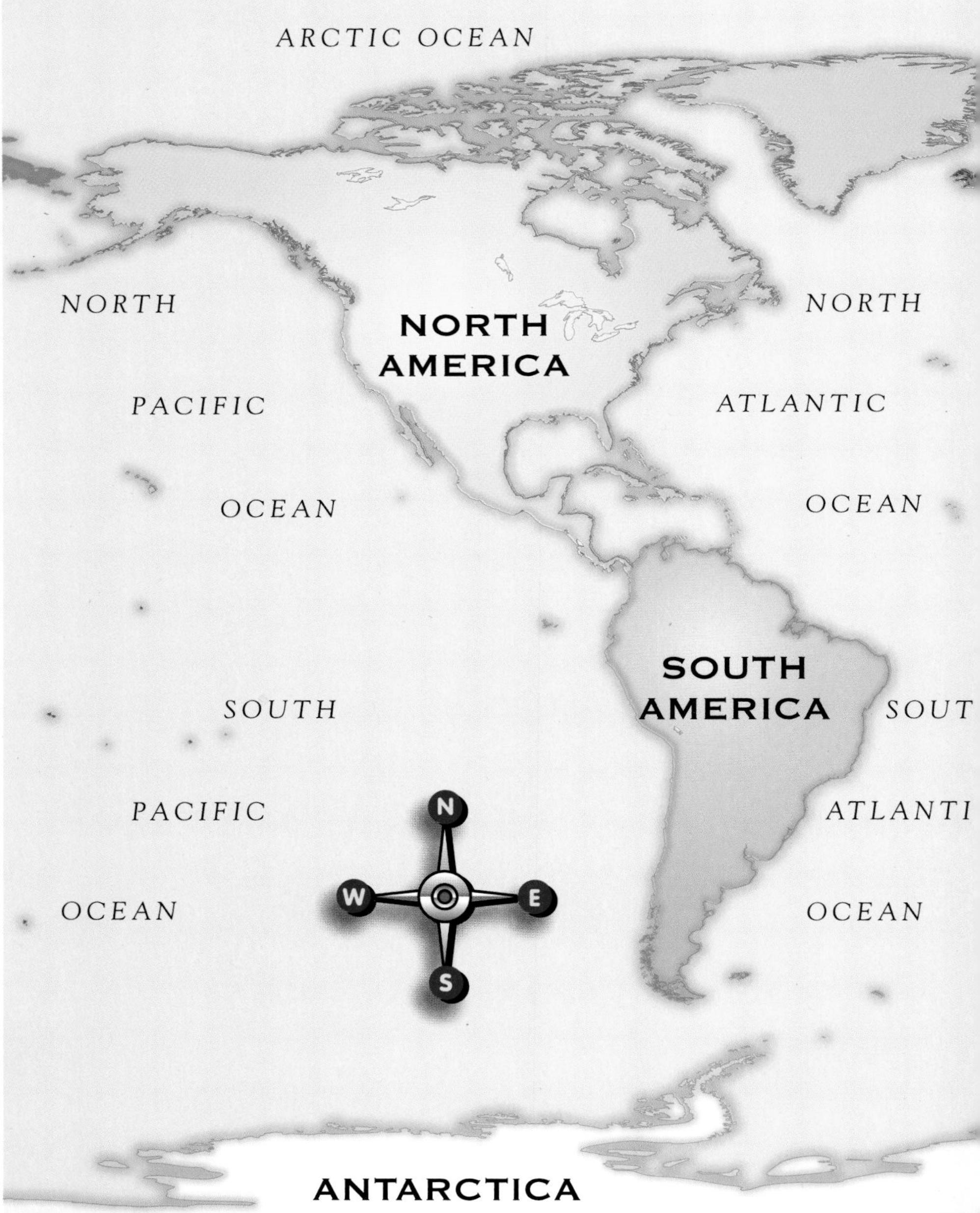

ARCTIC OCEAN

NORTH

PACIFIC

OCEAN

NORTH
AMERICA

SOUTH

PACIFIC

OCEAN

NORTH

ATLANTIC

OCEAN

SOUTH
AMERICA

SOUT

ATLANTI

OCEAN

N

W   E

S

ANTARCTICA

THE WORLD

ARCTIC OCEAN

EUROPE

ASIA

AFRICA

PACIFIC

OCEAN

INDIAN

OCEAN

AUSTRALIA

ANTARCTICA

Did You Know?

The Earth is covered with 71% water and only 29% land.

If you could drive around the earth's equator at 30 miles per hour, it would take you almost 35 days.

The center of the Earth is hotter than the surface of the Sun.

The Earth is over 4 billion years old.

The Earth's winds carry over 100 tons of sand around the world yearly. That means if you live in the United States, you could have sand from the Sahara Desert in your own backyard!

The Earth travels through space at about 66,700 miles per hour.

All 7 continents used to be part of one giant continent called Pangea.

The Earth is about 93 million miles away from the Sun.

The Earth's surface is made up of plates that are moving constantly. Each plate moves about 2 inches per year, and when they bump into each other it can cause earthquakes.

The Earth's oceans are an average of 2 miles deep.